We're from Mexico

Victoria Parker

Welcome to Mexico!

Heinemann Library
Chicago, Illinois

Customer Service   888-454-2279
Visit our website at www.heinemannlibrary.com

Photo research by Maria Joannou
Photography by John Millar
Designed by Ron Kamen and Celia Jones
Printed and bound in China by South China Printing Company

09 08 07 06 05
10 9 8 7 6 5 4 3 2 1

Library of Congress Cataloging-in-Publication Data
Parker, Victoria.
   We're from Mexico / Victoria Parker.
      p. cm. -- (We're from)
   ISBN 1-4034-5787-5 (library binding-hardcover) -- ISBN 1-4034-5794-8 (pbk.) 1. Mexico--Social life and customs--Juvenile literature. 2. Children--Mexico--Juvenile literature. 3. Family--Mexico--Juvenile literature. I. Title. II. Series.
   F1210.P272 2005
   972--dc22
                              2004017977

Acknowledgments
The author and publisher are grateful to the following for permission to reproduce copyright material:
Corbis/Royalty Free pp. 4a, 4b, 30c; John Millar pp. 1, 5a, 5b, 5c, 6, 7a, 7b, 8, 9, 10a, 11, 12, 13, 14, 15, 16, 17a, 17b, 18a, 18b, 19, 20, 21a, 21b, 22, 23, 24, 25a, 25b, 26, 27a, 27b, 28, 29a, 29b, 30a, 30b.

Cover photograph of Mexican school girls, reproduced with permission of John Millar. Many thanks to Nayeli, Luis, Raul, and their families.

Some words are shown in bold, **like this**. You can find out what they mean by looking in the glossary.

Contents

Where Is Mexico?

To learn about Mexico we meet three children who live there. Mexico is a very large country. It is south of the United States.

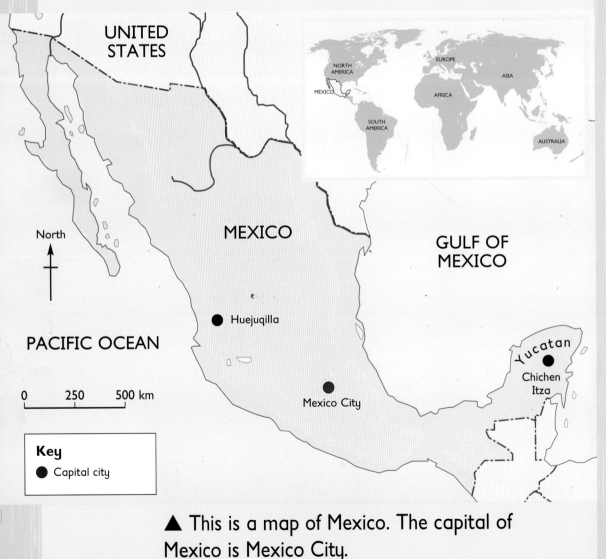

▲ This is a map of Mexico. The capital of Mexico is Mexico City.

◀ Mexico has many mountains.

There are hot, ▶ wet **rain forests** in southern Mexico.

◀ There are hot, dry **deserts** in northern Mexico.

5

Meet Nayeli

Nayeli is eight years old. She lives in Mexico City, the capital of Mexico. She lives with her parents, her twin brother Abraham, and her two dogs Gigo and Toby.

Nayeli

Abraham

Nayeli's father works in an office. He also owns three taxis. The family lives in a big house with Nayeli's aunt, uncle, and baby cousin.

Nayeli's parents

Nayeli's house ▶ has five bedrooms and a yard.

Nayeli at School

Nayeli enjoys school. She likes her uniform and her brightly painted classroom. She wants to be a teacher when she grows up.

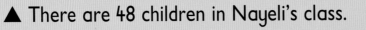
▲ There are 48 children in Nayeli's class.

School starts at 9.00 A.M. and finishes at 2.00 P.M. Nayeli and her friends have a half-hour break for lunch.

▲ Nayeli likes jam sandwiches, fruit, ice cream, and cola.

Nayeli's Home Life

After school, Nayeli and her friend Abigail do their homework. Then they play basketball, go to the park, or watch a movie.

Abigail

On weekends, Nayeli does jobs at home for her mother. She likes to help with the cooking.

▲ Nayeli cooks breakfast for her family.

The People and the Land

Mexico City is the biggest city in the world. It is on a high **plain** in the middle of Mexico. This is where most Mexicans live.

▲ More that fifteen million people live in Mexico City.

Mexico has many **volcanoes.**
Sometimes they **erupt.** Earthquakes
and hurricanes can happen, too. These
damage the land and people's homes.

Meet Luis

Luis is six years old. He comes from Huejuqilla. Huejuqilla is a small village in the mountains. He lives with his mother, two grandmothers, and his older brother and sister.

Luis's mother

Luis's grandmothers

Luis

14

There are not many jobs where Luis lives. Luis's father has gone to work in the United States. He comes home at Easter and Christmas.

▲ The main type of work around Luis's village is **cattle ranching.**

Luis's Home

Luis lives in a small house with two bedrooms. In the little kitchen, Luis's mother cooks food. She sells it in the school shop.

▲ Luis and his sister, Yensenia, like helping in the kitchen.

In their yard, Luis's family grows plants
and have a sink for washing. They
keep their pets there, too. They have
three cats, two dogs and a pigeon!

Luis's Day

Every morning, it is Luis's job to clean up the house and sweep the yard. Then he plays with his toy cars or his soccer ball.

▲ There are nineteen children in Luis's class.
They do not wear school uniforms.

In the afternoon, Luis goes to school. Sometimes his class watches television programs of lessons that are made in Mexico City.

Sundays in Mexico

On Sundays, most people in Mexico put on their best clothes and go to church.

Afterward, they often do something fun.
They might go out for a meal . . .

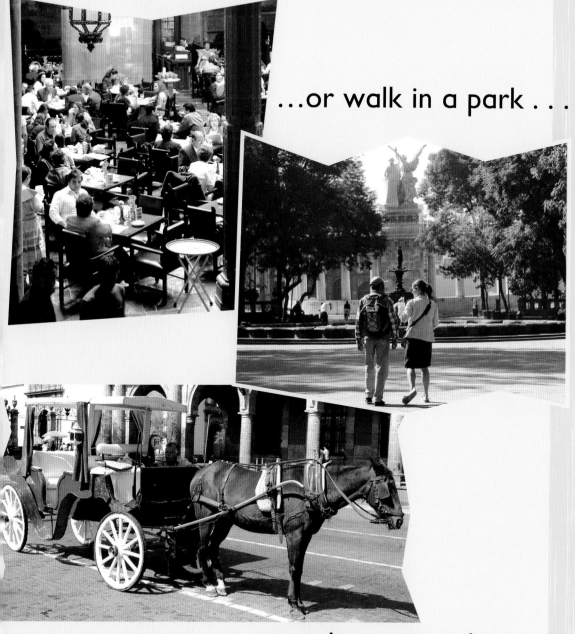

. . .or walk in a park . . .

. . .or take a special trip.

21

Meet Raul

Raul is eight years old. He comes from a seaside village in Yucatan. Raul lives with his parents and his older brother and sister.

▲ Yucatan is very hot. People sleep in **hammocks** because hammocks are cooler than beds.

Raul's home is all on one level. It has three bedrooms, a living room, a dining room, a kitchen, and a shower room.

Gone Fishing

Every family in Raul's village owns a boat. Raul's father takes his boat out each day to go fishing. On weekends, Raul helps him.

▲ Raul is learning how to be a fisher like his dad.

Raul's father sells most of the fish he catches. But he brings some home for the family to eat, too.

Raul's Daily Jobs

On weekdays, Raul goes to school from 7.00 A.M. until noon. In the afternoons, he does a job. He bikes around selling cakes for the village bakery.

On Sundays, Raul helps at church as
an **altar boy.** He prays for help with
his lessons and for his father to catch
lots of fish.

▲ Raul spends
his spare time
with his guitar
and his pets.

Mexico's History

People have lived in Mexico for thousands of years. Some of the people who lived in Mexico long ago were the Toltecs, Maya, and Aztecs. They built huge stone cities that you can still visit today.

▲ The Maya built this **temple** in a city called Chichen Itza.

About 500 years ago, Spanish people arrived in Mexico. They took charge of the country for 300 years. Today the main language of Mexico is Spanish.

▲ Spanish people made many buildings in Mexico City. ▶

Mexican Fact File

Flag   Capital City   Money

Mexico City

Peso

Religion
- Most people in Mexico are Roman Catholics.

Language
- The main language is Spanish. There are over 50 other languages spoken in different parts of the country.

Try speaking Spanish!
hola .... *hello*
que pasa? .... *how are you?*
gracias .... *thank you*

Glossary

altar boy boy who helps in church

cattle ranching job of herding cows over a huge area of land

desert very hot, dry area of land that has almost no rain and very few plants

erupt to burst out of

hammock net that hangs off the floor for people to lie in

plain large, flat, grassy area of land with few trees

rain forest thick forest of tall trees that grows in a hot, rainy place

temple where people go to pray

volcano mountain that has a hole down into Earth. Sometimes melted rock and ash erupt from it.

More Books to Read

Furlong, Kate A. *Mexico*. London: Checkerboard Books, 2000.

Hall, Margaret. *Around the World: Schools*. Chicago: Heinemann Library, 2002.

Foster, Leila and Fox, Mary. *Continents: South American*. Chicago: Heinemann Library, 2002.

Index